Write-and-Learn
Number
Practice Pages

S C H O L A S T I C
PROFESSIONAL**B**OOKS

New York • Toronto • London • Auckland • Sydney • New Delhi
Mexico City • Hong Kong • Buenos Aires

Coordinated by Rebecca Callan
Cover design by Norma Ortiz
Cover and interior artwork by Jane Dipold
Interior design by Norma Ortiz

ISBN: 0-439-45865-X
Copyright © 2003 Scholastic Inc.
All rights reserved. Published by Scholastic Inc.
Printed in the U.S.A.

2 3 4 5 6 7 8 9 10   40   09 08 07 06 05 04 03

Contents

• Introduction •

Welcome to *Write-and-Learn Number Practice Pages*! These ready-to-go pages introduce and reinforce each numeral and number word from 1 to 30. They also ensure kids get lots of practice counting and writing the featured numeral and number word.

Research shows that automatic number recognition is a critical element for math success. Though children will naturally develop their own handwriting style as they become more confident, all kids need to learn the basic strokes (and sequence of strokes) involved in each numeral and number word's formation. In this way, tracing and copying rows of numerals and number words strengthens learning and provides kinesthetic reinforcement.

Use the practice pages for whole-group, small-group, or individual work. You might also:

- give practice pages to children to complete at home

- put copies of the pages in a writing or math center

- have children create folders in which they collect their complete sheets and bind into a book when all thirty pages have been completed

- include the pages in children's portfolios

Using These Practice Pages

The practice page follows the same format and children complete each page the same way.

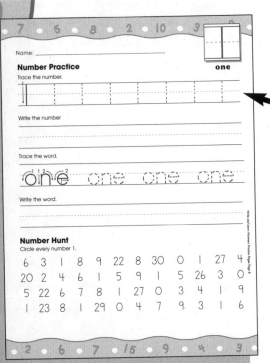

In the Number Practice section they:

- trace the numeral along guiding gray lines several times as they say it aloud (so that they have an auditory experience as well as a visual one). Children might begin by writing the numeral in the air.

- write the numeral themselves.

- trace the number word along guiding gray lines several times as they say it aloud (so that they have an auditory experience as well as a visual one). Children might even begin by writing the word in the air.

- write the number word themselves.

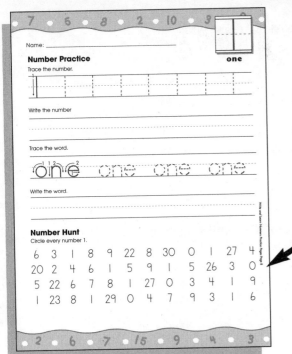

In the Number Hunt section they:

- find and then circle the target numeral, discriminating between commonly confused numerals and building faster number recognition.

In the Counting Practice section they:

- cut out the picture cards along the dotted lines at the bottom of the page and then glue the correct number in the designated area. Doing this gives them a hands-on experience with counting and provides practice reading the number word.

- follow the directions and draw the same number of pictures as the sentence indicates.

How to Use This Book

Procedures for Enhancing Number Learning

You might follow these steps for each numeral:

1. Preview the numeral you will introduce by writing it on the board or chart paper. Then give each child a page. Ask them to identify the numeral they see at the top.

2. Together, examine the numeral children will be practicing. Again, demonstrate the numeral on the board and narrate its formation ("The numeral 1 starts at the top and makes a stick straight down").

3. Have children "air trace" the numeral in the air.

4. Children can then trace and write the numerals on the lines using pencil. Point out the guide numbers and the arrows.

5. Have children complete one row of the numeral, compare it to the model, and then circle their best letter in the row.

You might follow these steps for each number word:

1. Preview the number word you will introduce by writing it on the board or chart paper. Ask them to identify the number word they see at the top of the page.

2. Together, examine the number word children will be practicing. Again, demonstrate the number word on the board and narrate its formation ("For the word one, the letter o curves around to the left, making a circle. The letter n . . .").

3. Have children "air trace" the letters of the number word in the air.

4. Children can then trace and write the number words on the lines using pencil. Point out the guide numbers and the arrows.

5. Have children complete one row of the number words, compare it to the model, and then circle their best number word in the row.

Number Activities

At the end of this book you'll find reproducible pages that can be used for practice:

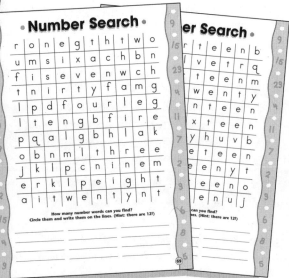

Search for Number Words (page 69–70)
Children search for number words and circle them. You can also make your own word searches with any number words you wish by using graph paper.

Number Bingo (page 71)
Have children randomly write a number from 1 to 30 in each square. Then, call out numbers one at a time. Have children put a marker or color the square with that number. The first child to get five across calls "bingo!" Children may also enjoy the leading the game.

Stationary (page 72)
You'll find reproducible stationary for any writing activity. Great for giving children practice forming numerals and writing number words.

Beyond the Practice Sheets

Extend math learning beyond the practice pages and invite children to experience numbers in a variety of ways! Here are a few ideas to get you started:

Concentration
On a set of index cards, write each numeral or number word twice (once per card). Children turn all the cards facedown and turn over two at a time, trying to make a match. If they do so, they keep the cards and take another turn; if they do not, they turn the cards back over and the next player has a turn.

Counting Cards
Make a set of cards children can use with manipulatives to practice counting. Write the numbers 1 to 30 (or number word) on large oaktag squares. On each square, place one-inch round stickers—the number of stickers will correspond to the numeral (or number word) written on the card. Distribute the cards and manipulatives to the children. Each child will need one card and access to as many as thirty manipulatives. (Plastic counters work well for this activity.) Ask children to place one manipulative on each sticker and then count the number of manipulatives on his or her square. (The number counted should equal the numeral (or number word) printed on the square. To check their work, invite children to then count the manipulatives on their squares with a friend.) To keep this activity fresh and fun, change the manipulatives regularly. You may want to use manipulatives that match the month, such as pumpkin seeds for October, candy hearts for February, and so on.

Messy Writing
Let children use their fingers to write letters in thin layers of shaving cream, finger paint, pudding, or whipped cream. Tape a large piece of waxed paper to a tabletop and spread the messy material thin. Then invite children to "write" with their index finger!

Counting Book Library
Set aside a special place for children to explore counting books. You may want to visit your local library from time to time to keep the supply interesting and engaging. Encourage children to pair up in partners. Have one partner be the "reader" who describes what he or she sees happening in each picture and one partner be the "counter" who uses his or her index finger to count the objects on the page. Then have the partners switch roles, so that each child has a turn being the "reader" and the "counter."

one

Name: _____

Number Practice

Trace the number.

Write the number.

Trace the word.

 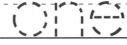 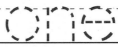 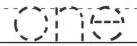

Write the word.

Number Hunt

Circle every number 1.

6	3	1	8	9	22	8	30	0	1	27	4
20	2	4	6	1	5	9	1	5	26	3	0
5	22	6	7	8	1	27	0	3	4	1	9
1	23	8	1	29	0	4	7	9	3	1	6

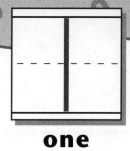

one

Name: _____

Cut out 1 sun. Paste it in the sky.

Draw 1 rainbow.

2

two

Number Practice

Trace the number.

2 2 2 2 2 2 2 2

Write the number.

Trace the word.

two two two two

Write the word.

Number Hunt

Circle every number 2.

13	0	4	6	19	2	30	2	0	17	6
2	9	3	14	0	2	11	5	6	15	3
17	3	2	6	16	8	10	7	9	2	3
19	2	18	9	5	4	2	0	1	16	18

Name: _____

Cut out 2 trees. Paste them on the hill.

Draw 2 birds in the nest.

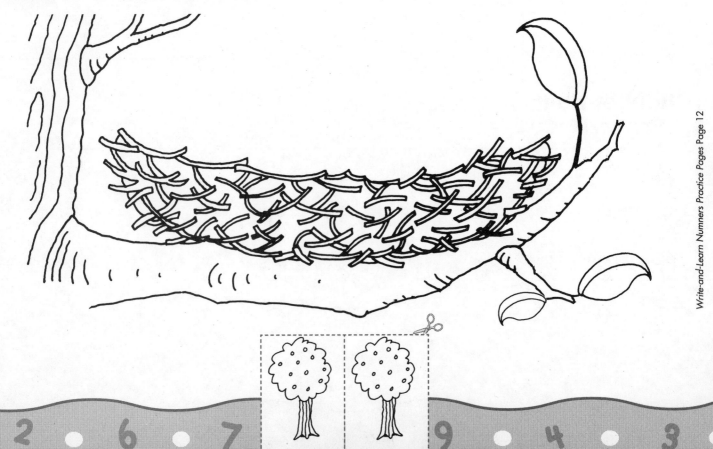

3

three

Name: _____

Number Practice

Trace the number.

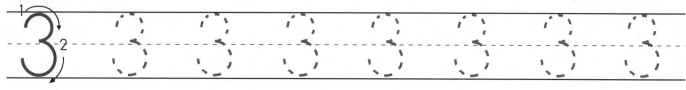

Write the number.

Trace the word.

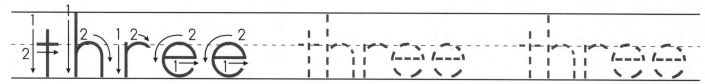

Write the word.

Number Hunt

Circle every number 3.

0	3	1	8	13	9	25	2	4	26	4
21	5	7	12	3	25	3	9	8	1	2
8	16	24	3	0	5	4	3	20	0	5
3	0	29	1	3	7	19	8	10	14	9

3

three

Name: _____

Cut out 3 goldfish. Paste them in the bowl.

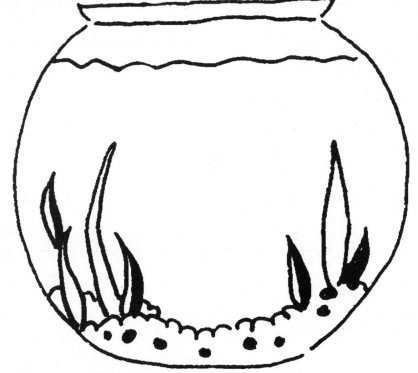

Draw 3 whales in the ocean.

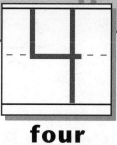

four

Name: _____

Number Practice

Trace the number.

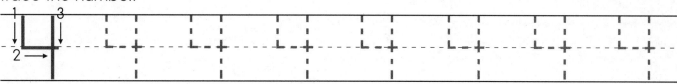

Write the number.

_____

- -

_____

Trace the word.

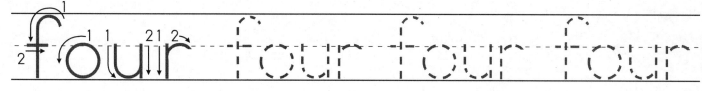

Write the word.

_____

- -

_____

Number Hunt

Circle every number 4.

30	16	25	4	6	3	18	0	9	27	29	0
1	10	20	1	5	10	4	6	9	6	22	26
5	18	21	4	13	5	28	4	9	0	11	12
7	26	4	6	3	7	22	7	8	9	29	6

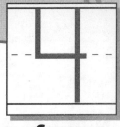

four

Name: _____

Cut out 4 crabs. Paste them on the beach.

Draw 4 beach balls.

five

Name: _____

Number Practice

Trace the number.

 5 5 5 5 5 5 5

Write the number.

_____

- -

_____

Trace the word.

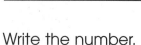 five five five

Write the word.

_____

- -

_____

Number Hunt

Circle every number 5.

2	5	3	0	I	4	5	8	9	6	10	5
6	4	18	5	2	I	7	5	0	9	5	3
7	3	8	I	9	5	16	7	0	I	4	5
11	4	5	9	21	3	9	2	I	10	8	7

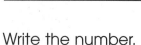

5

five

Name: _____

Cut out 5 butterflies. Paste them in the garden.

Draw 5 ladybugs on the leaf.

six

Name: _____

Number Practice

Trace the number.

 6 6 6 6 6 6 6

Write the number.

_____

- - - - - - - - - - - - - - - - - - - -

_____

Trace the word.

six   six   six   six   six

Write the word.

_____

- - - - - - - - - - - - - - - - - - - -

_____

Number Hunt

Circle every number 6.

0	2	1	8	13	9	25	2	6	20	5	4
28	6	7	12	9	25	3	6	8	1	9	3
6	17	2	6	3	0	5	6	3	20	0	2
0	29	1	3	7	19	8	10	1	6	8	6

6

six

Name: _____

Cut out 6 frogs. Paste them on the log.

Draw 6 flies for the frogs to eat.

7

seven

Name: _____

Number Practice

Trace the number.

7 / / / / / / / /

Write the number.

Trace the word.

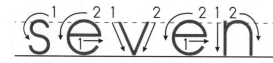 seven seven

Write the word.

Number Hunt

Circle every number 7.

5	7	1	8	13	9	25	7	4	26	7
11	5	7	12	3	25	3	9	8	1	4
2	16	24	3	7	5	4	3	20	0	9
8	7	29	1	3	7	19	8	10	14	5

Name: _____

Cut out 7 lollipops. Paste them in the candy jar.

Draw 7 candles on the cake.

eight

Name: _____

Number Practice

Trace the number.

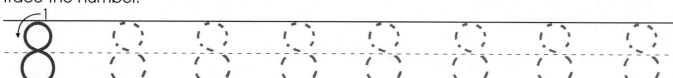

Write the number.

Trace the word.

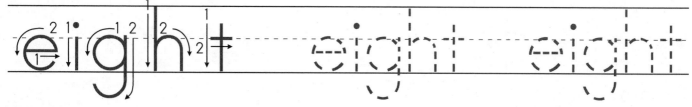

Write the word.

Number Hunt

Circle every number 8.

9	25	2	4	26	8	13	4	0	8	1
12	3	25	3	9	21	5	7	8	1	2
24	8	0	5	4	3	20	0	5	8	16
1	8	7	19	8	10	14	9	3	0	29

8
eight

Name: _____

Cut out 8 lizards. Paste them on the rock.

Draw 8 spiders on the web.

q

nine

Name: _____

Number Practice

Trace the number.

q q q q q q q q

Write the number.

Trace the word.

nine nine nine nine

Write the word.

Number Hunt

Circle every number 9.

9	3	1	8	13	9	25	2	4	26	4
8	1	2	21	5	7	12	3	25	3	9
0	9	4	3	20	0	9	8	16	24	3
1	7	20	8	10	3	0	2	9	14	9

Name: _____

Cut out 9 sheep. Paste them in the field.

Draw 9 clouds in the sky.

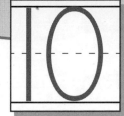

ten

Name: _____

Number Practice

Trace the number.

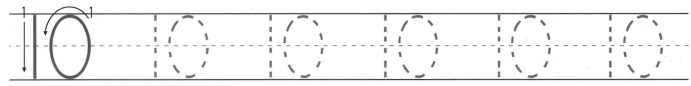

Write the number.

_____

- -

_____

Trace the word.

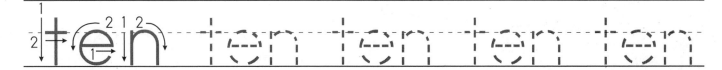

Write the word.

_____

- -

_____

Number Hunt

Circle every number 10.

2	4	26	40	3	1	8	10	9	25	10
10	25	3	9	8	1	2	21	5	7	12
3	0	5	4	3	10	0	5	8	10	24
7	10	8	10	14	9	3	0	29	1	3

10

ten

Name: _____

Cut out 10 owls. Paste them on the branches.

Draw 10 bats in the cave.

11
eleven

Name: _____

Number Practice

Trace the number.

Write the number.

_____

- - - - - - - - - - - - - - - - - - - -

_____

Trace the word.

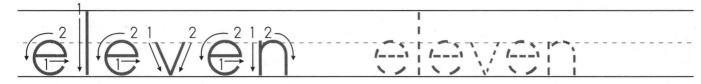

Write the word.

_____

- - - - - - - - - - - - - - - - - - - -

_____

Number Hunt

Circle every number 11.

9	25	2	4	26	4	0	3	1	11	13
11	3	25	3	9	8	11	2	21	5	7
3	0	5	4	3	20	0	5	8	11	24
1	3	7	11	8	10	14	9	3	11	29

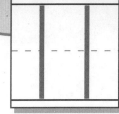

eleven

Name: _____

Cut out 11 pennies. Paste them in the piggybank.

Draw 11 windows on the building.

twelve

Number Practice

Trace the number.

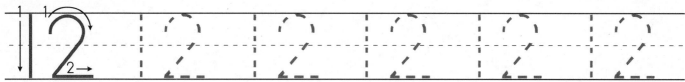

Write the number.

Trace the word.

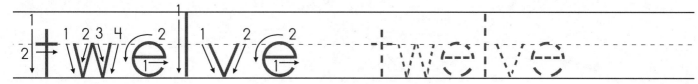

Write the word.

Number Hunt

Circle every number 12.

8	13	0	3	12	9	25	12	4	26	4
12	25	3	9	8	1	2	21	5	7	22
24	3	12	5	4	3	20	0	5	8	16
3	0	29	12	8	10	14	9	3	12	19

Name: _____

Cut out 12 apples. Paste them on the tree.

Draw 12 flowers.

13

thirteen

Name: _____

Number Practice

Trace the number.

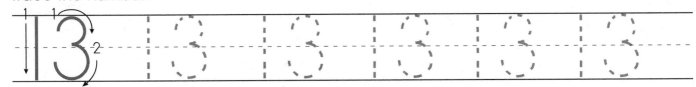

Write the number.

_____

- - - - - - - - - - - - - - - - - - -

_____

Trace the word.

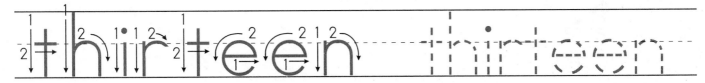

Write the word.

_____

- - - - - - - - - - - - - - - - - - -

_____

Number Hunt

Circle every number 13.

9	25	2	13	26	4	0	13	1	8	13
21	5	7	3	9	8	1	2	12	3	25
16	13	20	13	5	24	3	0	5	4	3
13	19	8	10	14	9	0	29	9	13	7

13
thirteen

Name: _____

Cut out 13 cupcakes. Paste them below.

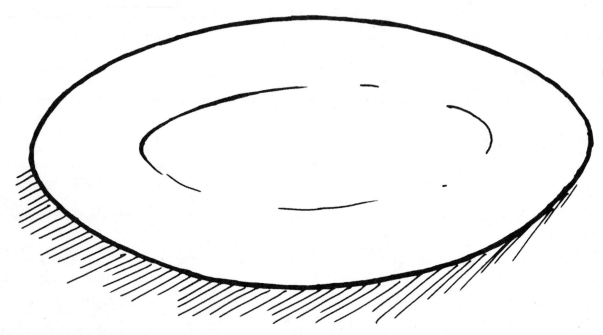

Draw 13 balloons for the party.

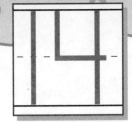

fourteen

Name: _____

Number Practice

Trace the number.

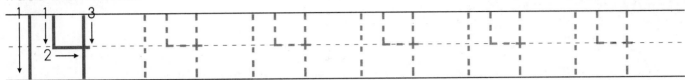

Write the number.

_____

- - - - - - - - - - - - - - - - - -

_____

Trace the word.

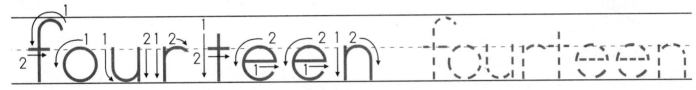

Write the word.

_____

- - - - - - - - - - - - - - - - - -

_____

Number Hunt

Circle every number 14.

0	14	1	8	13	9	25	2	4	26	14
21	5	7	14	3	25	3	9	8	14	2
8	14	24	3	0	5	14	3	20	0	5
3	0	29	14	3	7	14	8	10	14	9

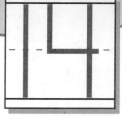

fourteen

Name: _____

Cut out 14 penguins. Paste them on the icebergs.

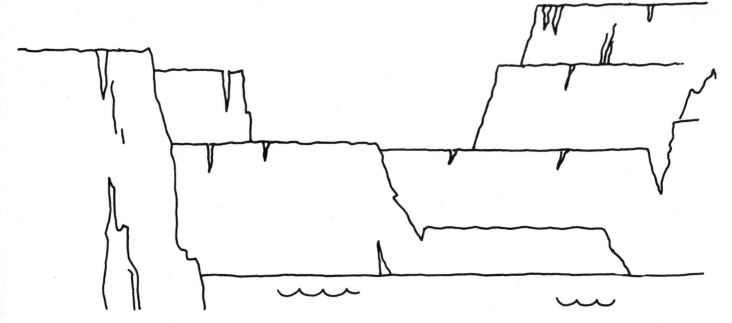

Draw 14 snowflakes in the sky.

fifteen

Name: _____

Number Practice

Trace the number.

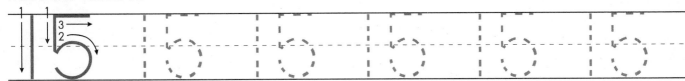

Write the number.

_____

- -

_____

Trace the word.

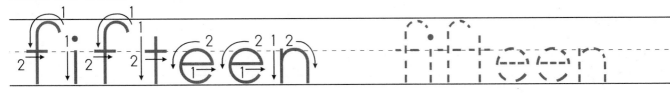

Write the word.

_____

- -

_____

Number Hunt

Circle every number 15.

8	13	9	25	15	4	26	4	0	3	1
25	15	9	8	1	2	21	5	7	15	3
5	4	3	20	15	5	8	16	24	3	0
15	3	7	19	8	10	15	9	3	0	16

fifteen

Name: _____

Cut out 15 chicks. Paste them in the barnyard.

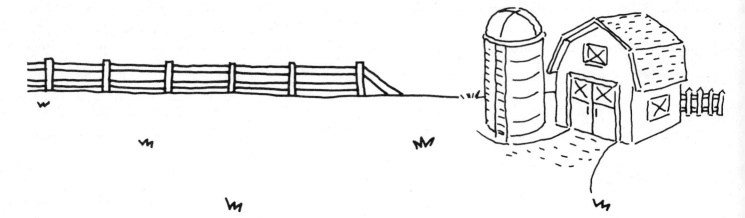

Draw 15 eggs.

Name: _____

Number Practice

Trace the number.

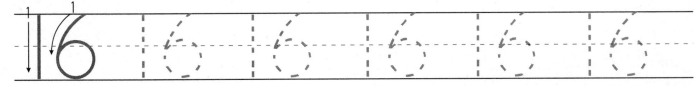

Write the number.

Trace the word.

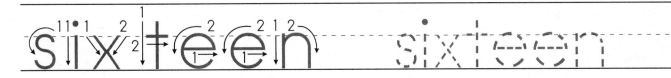

Write the word.

Number Hunt

Circle every number 16.

10	16	9	8	13	9	25	2	16	26	4
21	5	16	12	3	25	3	9	5	16	3
16	0	5	8	16	24	3	0	16	1	2
3	0	29	16	3	7	19	8	0	3	16

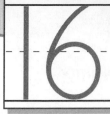

sixteen

Name: _____

Cut out 16 turtles. Paste them on the rocks.

Draw 16 squares on the turtle shell.

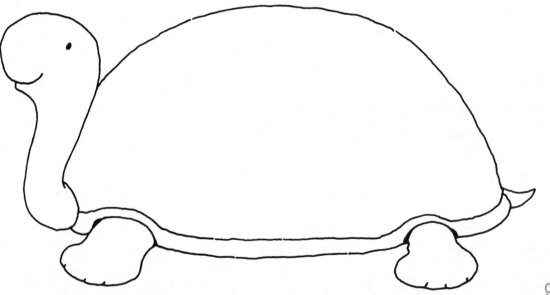

Write-and-Learn Numbers Practice Pages Page 40

17

seventeen

Name: _____

Number Practice

Trace the number.

Write the number.

_____

- -

_____

Trace the word.

_____

seventeen

Write the word.

_____

- -

_____

Number Hunt

Circle every number 17.

17	3	1	8	13	9	25	2	17	26	4
21	17	7	12	3	25	3	9	8	1	17
8	16	24	3	0	17	4	3	20	0	5
3	17	29	1	3	7	17	8	10	14	17

17
seventeen

Name: _____

Cut out 17 seahorses. Paste them in the water.

Draw 17 clams on the beach.

18
eighteen

Name: _____

Number Practice

Trace the number.

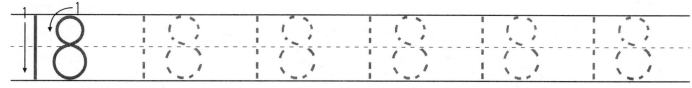

Write the number.

_____

- - - - - - - - - - - - - - - - - - - -

_____

Trace the word.

Write the word.

_____

- - - - - - - - - - - - - - - - - - - -

_____

Number Hunt

Circle every number 18.

2	16	24	18	0	5	4	3	20	18	5
0	3	1	8	13	9	25	2	4	26	18
18	0	29	1	3	7	19	8	18	14	9
21	18	7	12	3	25	3	9	8	18	2

18

eighteen

Name: _____

Cut out 18 pretzels. Paste them on the plate.

Draw 18 pieces of popcorn.

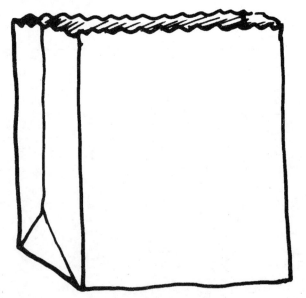

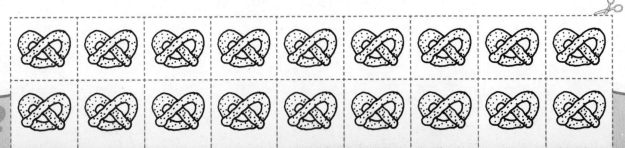

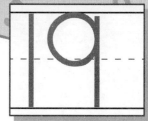

nineteen

Name: _____

Number Practice

Trace the number.

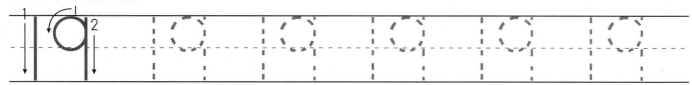

Write the number.

_____

- - - - - - - - - - - - - - - -

_____

Trace the word.

_____

Write the word.

_____

- - - - - - - - - - - - - - - -

_____

Number Hunt

Circle every number 19.

19	5	7	12	3	25	3	19	8	1	2
9	25	2	4	26	4	19	3	1	8	13
8	19	24	3	0	5	4	3	20	0	19
7	19	0	29	1	19	7	19	8	10	14

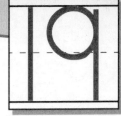

nineteen

Name: _____

Cut out 19 strawberries. Paste them in the bowl.

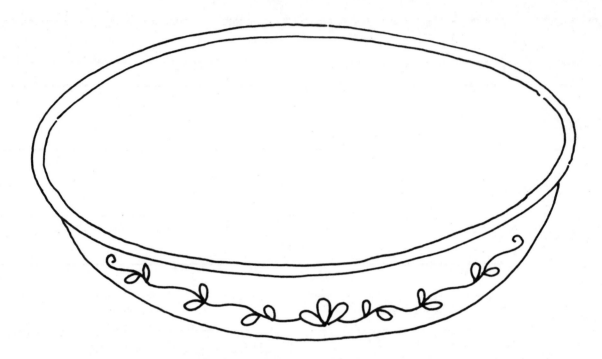

Draw 19 ants in the grass.

Name: _____

Number Practice

Trace the number.

Write the number.

_____

- - - - - - - - - - - - - - - - -

_____

Trace the word.

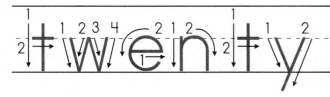   twenty

Write the word.

_____

- - - - - - - - - - - - - - - - -

_____

Number Hunt

Circle every number 20.

20	0	29	1	3	7	19	20	10	14	9
21	5	7	12	20	25	3	9	8	1	20
8	20	24	3	0	5	4	20	20	0	5
0	3	1	20	13	9	25	2	4	26	20

Name: _____

Cut out 20 dragonflies. Paste them above the pond.

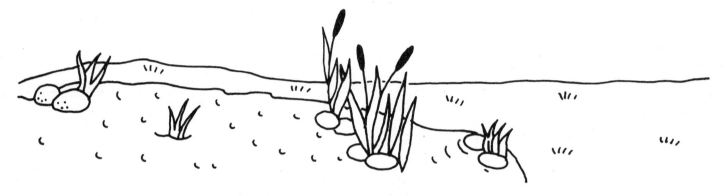

Draw 20 fish swimming.

twenty-one

Number Practice

Trace the number.

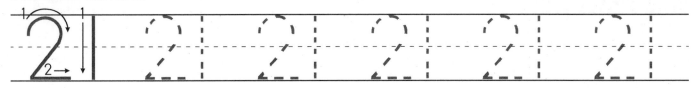

Write the number.

Trace the word.

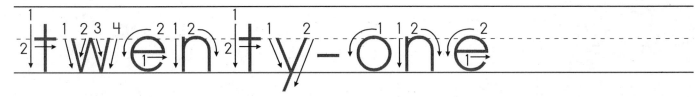

Write the word.

Number Hunt

Circle every number 21.

0	3	21	8	13	9	5	3	9	8	21	2
21	5	2	4	26	4	21	7	1	3	6	7
16	5	4	3	21	0	5	19	8	10	21	8
3	0	21	1	3	7	14	9	21	3	0	4

21

twenty-one

Name: _____

Cut out 21 grasshoppers. Paste them in the meadow.

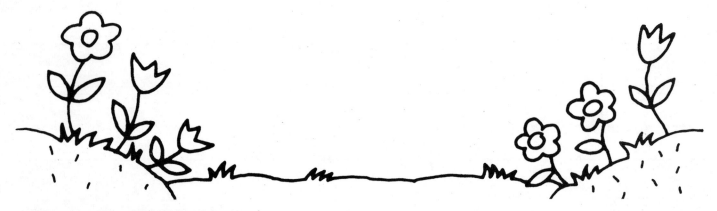

Draw 21 kites flying.

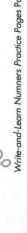

22
twenty-two

Number Practice

Trace the number.

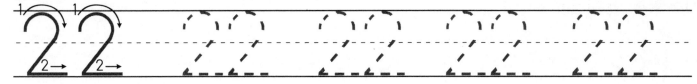

Write the number.

Trace the word.

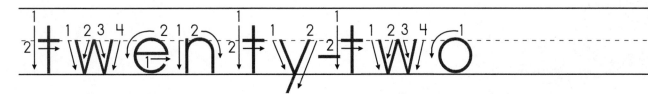

Write the word.

Number Hunt

Circle every number 22.

0	3	22	8	13	9	25	2	4	26	22
1	22	21	5	22	12	3	25	3	9	8
8	22	24	3	0	5	4	3	22	0	22
3	0	29	1	22	7	19	8	10	14	9

Name: _____

Cut out 22 fireflies. Paste them in the sky.

Draw 22 stars.

twenty-three

Name: _____

Number Practice

Trace the number.

Write the number.

_____

- -

_____

Trace the word.

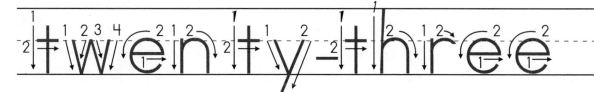

Write the word.

_____

- -

_____

Number Hunt

Circle every number 23.

3	0	29	1	3	7	19	8	10	9	22
9	23	2	4	26	4	0	3	23	8	13
23	8	16	24	30	5	4	3	23	0	5
21	5	7	12	0	25	23	9	8	1	23

Name: _____

Cut out 23 mice. Paste them in the barnyard.

Draw 23 pieces of cheese.

twenty-four

Name: _____

Number Practice

Trace the number.

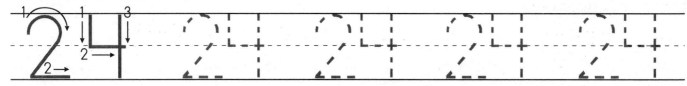

Write the number.

_____

- -

_____

Trace the word.

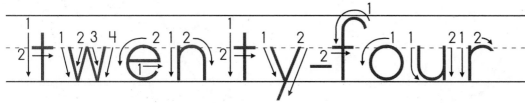

Write the word.

_____

- -

_____

Number Hunt

Circle every number 24.

0	24	1	8	13	9	25	2	4	26	4
24	5	7	12	3	24	3	9	8	1	2
8	16	24	3	0	5	24	3	20	0	5
3	0	24	1	3	7	19	8	10	24	9

Name: _____

Cut out 24 cookies. Paste them in the jar.

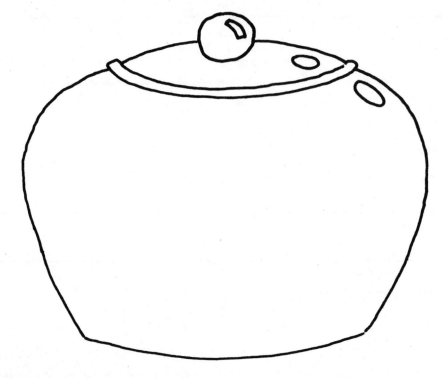

Draw 24 donuts on the plate.

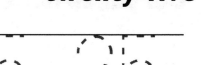
twenty-five

Number Practice

Trace the number.

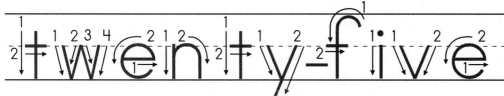

Write the number.

Trace the word.

twenty-five

Write the word.

Number Hunt

Circle every number 25.

8	16	25	3	0	5	4	3	25	0	5
0	3	1	8	13	9	25	2	25	26	4
21	25	7	12	3	25	3	9	8	1	2
3	0	25	1	3	7	19	25	10	14	9

Name: _____

Cut out 25 leaves. Paste them below.

Draw 25 ice cream scoops on the plate.

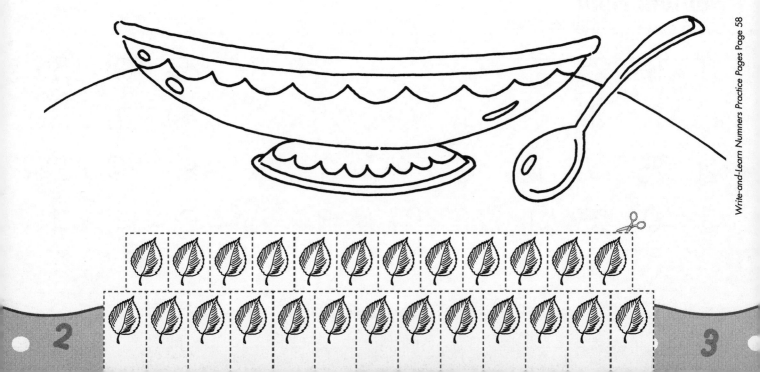

twenty-six

Name: _____

Number Practice

Trace the number.

 26 26 26 26 26

Write the number.

Trace the word.

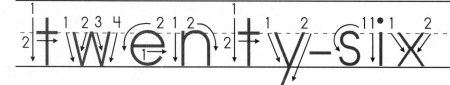

Write the word.

Number Hunt

Circle every number 26.

9	25	2	4	26	4	0	3	1	8	13	26
26	9	8	1	2	26	1	3	7	19	3	7
8	26	5	4	3	20	0	5	24	3	0	26
3	0	26	10	26	14	9	21	5	7	12	8

Name: _____

Cut out 26 birds. Paste them above the field.

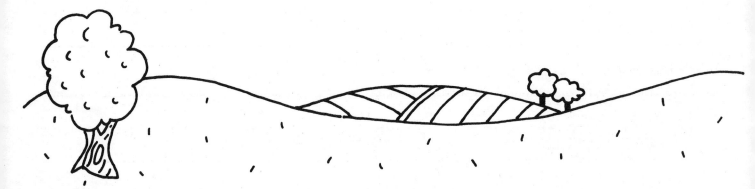

Draw 26 raindrops under the clouds.

27
twenty-seven

Name: _____

Number Practice

Trace the number.

2 7 27 27 27 27

Write the number.

Trace the word.

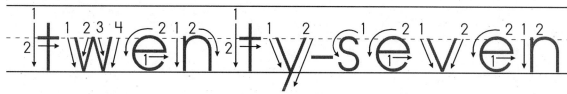
twenty-seven

Write the word.

Number Hunt

Circle every number 27.

7	3	1	8	273	9	25	2	4	27	4
27	5	7	12	3	27	3	9	8	1	2
8	16	27	3	0	5	4	3	27	0	5
3	0	27	1	3	27	19	8	10	27	9

27

twenty-seven

Name: _____

Cut out 27 crayons. Paste them below.

Draw 27 hairs on the head.

28
twenty-eight

Name: _____

Number Practice

Trace the number.

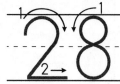 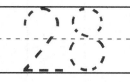   

Write the number.

_____

- -

_____

Trace the word.

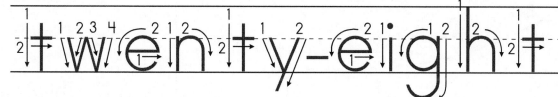

Write the word.

_____

- -

_____

Number Hunt

Circle every number 28.

7	19	8	10	28	9	0	3	2	4	26
28	16	24	3	0	5	28	3	20	0	5
21	5	7	12	28	25	3	9	28	1	2
3	0	28	1	3	1	28	13	9	25	28

Name: _____

Cut out 28 jellybeans. Paste them in the bowl.

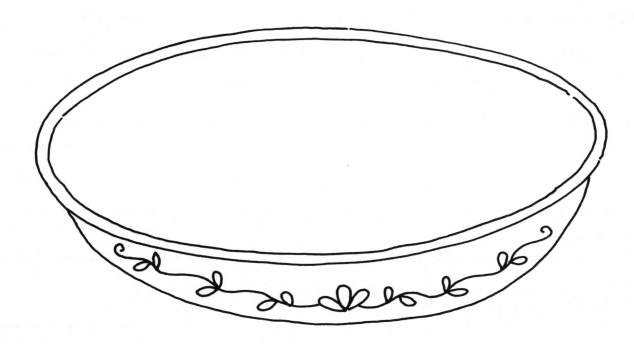

Draw 28 polka dots on the pillow.

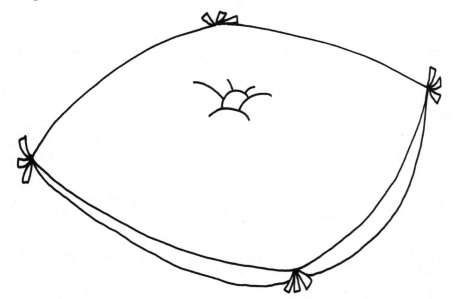

29

twenty-nine

Name: _____

Number Practice

Trace the number.

Write the number.

Trace the word.

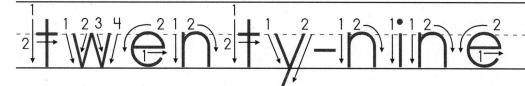

Write the word.

Number Hunt

Circle every number 29.

0	29	9	1	8	13	29	25	2	4	26	4
21	5	7	12	3	29	3	9	8	1	29	10
8	29	16	24	3	0	5	4	3	29	0	5
3	0	29	1	3	7	19	8	10	14	29	8

Name: _____

Cut out 29 bees. Paste them near their hive.

Draw 29 blades of grass in the field.

Write-and-Learn Numners Practice Pages Page 66

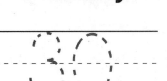

thirty

Number Practice

Trace the number.

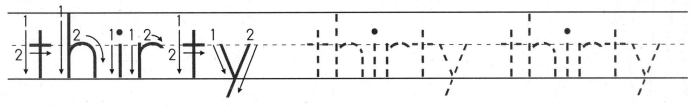

Write the number.

Trace the word.

Write the word.

Number Hunt

Circle every number 30.

0	30	1	8	13	9	25	2	30	26	4
21	5	7	12	30	25	30	9	8	1	2
8	16	24	30	0	5	4	3	20	30	5
30	0	29	1	30	7	19	8	10	14	9

30
thirty

Name: _____

Cut out 30 paw prints. Paste them below.

Draw 30 stripes on the tiger.

•Number Search•

r	o	n	e	g	t	h	t	w	o
u	m	s	i	x	a	c	h	b	n
f	i	s	e	v	e	n	w	c	h
t	n	i	r	t	y	f	a	m	g
l	p	d	f	o	u	r	l	e	g
l	t	e	n	g	b	f	i	r	e
p	q	a	l	g	b	h	l	a	k
o	b	n	m	l	t	h	r	e	e
j	k	l	p	c	n	i	n	e	m
e	r	k	l	p	e	i	g	h	t
a	i	t	w	e	n	t	y	n	t

How many number words can you find?
Circle them and write them on the lines. (Hint: There are 12!)

_____   _____   _____

_____   _____   _____

_____   _____   _____

_____   _____   _____

69

• Number Search •

q	t	h	i	r	t	e	e	n	b
w	t	w	e	l	v	e	t	r	q
y	f	o	u	r	t	e	e	n	m
o	n	e	w	t	w	e	n	t	y
o	s	e	v	e	n	t	e	e	n
n	m	k	s	i	x	t	e	e	n
t	h	i	r	t	y	h	u	v	b
c	v	n	i	n	e	t	e	e	n
e	i	g	h	t	e	e	n	y	t
u	z	f	i	f	t	e	e	n	o
r	h	e	l	e	v	e	n	u	j

How many number words can you find?
Circle them and write them on the lines. (Hint: There are 12!)

_____   _____   _____

_____   _____   _____

_____   _____   _____

• Number Bingo •